Not 1, not 2 but...

21

Ways to Improve Your Emotional Intelligence

A Practical Approach

Hank Clemons, PhD

SoEI
P.O. Box 341738 – Tampa, FL 33694
www.societyofei.com

21
Ways to Improve Your Emotional Intelligence

ISBN: 978-1-63263-558-7

Published by BookLocker.com, Inc., Bradenton, Florida.

Printed in the United States of America on acid-free paper.

If you give any type of medical, legal or professional advice, you must also include a disclaimer. You can find examples of these online using your favorite search engine. Most professional websites that offer advice have these types of disclaimers.

Library of Congress Control Number: 2014918747

1. Leadership
2. Interpersonal Skills
3. Self-help

BookLocker.com, Inc.
2015

First Edition

Emotional Intelligence is a practice…,
not just a term.

For information, contact:
Dr. Hank at SoEI
P.O. Box 341738
Tampa, FL 33694

DISCLAIMER

This book details the author's personal experiences with and opinions about emotional intelligence. The author is not licensed psychologist.

The author and publisher are providing this book and its contents on an "as is" basis and make no representations or warranties of any kind with respect to this book or its contents. The author and publisher disclaim all such representations and warranties, including for example warranties of merchantability and medical or legal advice for a particular purpose. In addition, the author and publisher do not represent or warrant that the information accessible via this book is accurate, complete or current.

The statements made about products and services have not been evaluated by the U.S. government. Please consult with your own legal or accounting professional regarding the suggestions and recommendations made in this book.

Except as specifically stated in this book, neither the author or publisher, nor any authors, contributors, or other representatives will be liable for damages arising out of or in connection with the use of this book. This is a comprehensive limitation of liability that applies to all damages of any kind, including (without limitation) compensatory; direct, indirect or consequential damages; loss of data, income or profit; loss of or damage to property and claims of third parties.

You understand that this book is not intended as a substitute for consultation with a licensed legal or accounting professional. Before you begin any change in your lifestyle in any way, you will consult a licensed professional to ensure that you are doing what's best for your situation.

This book provides content related to emotional intelligence topics. As such, use of this book implies your acceptance of this disclaimer.

Acknowledgements

I'd like to acknowledge four very special people that I miss and were a big part of who I am today. Not by their name, which is not nearly as important as their relationship to me – my father, mother, brother and sister.

CONTENTS

Read this First!

The key skills of emotional intelligence can be learned by anyone, at any time. There is a difference, however, between learning about emotional intelligence and applying that knowledge to your personal and professional life. Just because you know you *should* do something doesn't mean you will—especially when you become overwhelmed by stress.

After reading this book, select one, only one of the ***21 ways*** to increase your emotional intelligence. After selecting the one you want to implement, use than action plan found in the last section or create an electronic one of your own using a similar format.

This book offers ***21 ways*** that you can work on your emotional intelligence so that you can begin to make a difference in your situation. Although each of the skills can help you in some way, you may find some skills more important than others, depending on your current situation.

Introduction

Emotions are a fundamental quality of human beings and represent an enormous untapped potential to produce business results by harnessing them in a positive and constructive way. Whether in relation to managing difficult or sensitive situations, dealing with colleagues or interacting with customers, the power of emotions to help achieve work goals and enhance academic and business success has been largely neglected up until now.

The concept of Emotional Intelligence (EI) provides a framework within which we can recognize and actively manage emotional behaviors. It can provide a way to improve performance in a wide range of people-based roles and situations.

So, unless you live or work in a vacuum, you have to deal with people -- all kinds of people.

Fortunately emotional intelligence can be learned and strengthened, *but only when an individual understands how emotional intelligence is observable and useful.* There is much literature and many tests available to help you determine your current EI and identify where you may need to do some work. Everyone has aspects of their lives that they can improve.

What is Emotional Intelligence?

Having the skill and ability to recognize, understand and manage our emotions and those of others to lead healthier, happier and more productive lives.

This is one of many definitions. If you're new to the field, you will discover many others as you read and hear more about the concept.

If you're experienced, you understand that the lack of a standardized definition is because the field is young and continues to evolve. However, there are several accepted concepts around emotional intelligence. One of them is that emotional intelligence consist of the following four elements:

- Self-awareness - You recognize your own emotions and how they affect your thoughts and behavior, know your strengths and weaknesses, and have self-confidence.
- Self-management - The ability to control impulsive feelings and behaviors, manage your emotions in healthy ways, take initiative, follow through on commitments, and adapt to changing circumstances.

- Social-awareness - Social awareness involves understanding the emotions, needs and concerns of other people. Social awareness incorporates the ability to empathize, which means sensing others' feelings and perspective, and taking an active interest in their concerns.
- Relationship Management - The ability to develop and maintain good relationships, communicate clearly, inspire and influence others, work well in a team, and manage conflict.

People with high emotional intelligence are usually successful in most things they do. Those that aren't are not.

As you've probably determined, emotional intelligence can be a key to success in your personal life and career as well. The ability to interact effectively with others, build and maintain relationships is very important, so developing and using your emotional intelligence is a must.

Everyone has aspects of their lives that they can improve.

The key skills of emotional intelligence can be learned by anyone, at any time. You can develop your emotional intelligence, but it will take persistence, focus and practice.

There is a difference, however, between learning about emotional intelligence and applying that knowledge to your life. Emotional Intelligence is a *practice*, not just a *term*.

1

Name that Feeling/Emotion

Why name that feeling/emotion? Descriptive words help us understand ourselves and the world around us. If we don't have enough names for our emotions, it's hard to get a handle on what we're feeling when an emotion arise.

People, who ignore, dismiss, repress or just vent their emotions, are setting themselves up for physical illness. Research has found that the effects of consistent emotion suppression include increased physical stress on your body, including high blood pressure, increased incidence of diabetes and heart disease. Also, people who regularly suppress emotions are often less aware of the signals they are sending to others and also less aware of the social cues present in daily conversation.

Emotions are reliable indicators of what is really going on inside of us. There are many ways to identify emotions and you will have to choose the manner that is most suitable to you. Recognizing and naming (identifying) emotions helps us build better relationships. That's because being aware of our emotions can help us talk about feelings more clearly, avoid or resolve conflicts better, and move past difficult feelings more easily.

Just how many emotions are there? Due to the sheer vastness and complexity involved, it is difficult to exactly define and enlist all the emotions experienced. Most researchers conclude that there are seven *basic* emotions. Basic emotions are emotions that have been scientifically proven to have a certain facial expression associated with it. For example, the basic emotion of "Anger" can be recognized all around the world, no matter what age, religion or gender you are, or what language you speak. Other basic emotions include, fear disgust, contempt, happiness, sadness and surprise.

Tips & Exercises

Learning to identify various emotions takes time. Expect to practice daily for months before you begin to notice a change in your ability to identify emotions. Here's an exercise that's designed to help you recognize the emotions you are having. Start small— do this exercise each day for even just a few seconds. The key is to build slowly over time, to practice with lots of different types of emotions, and to be consistent in the (daily) practice.

1. Sit for a moment and pay attention to your physical sensations and thoughts. See if you can give an emotion you are having a name (e.g., cheerful, anger, shame).
2. Once you have a name for the emotion, write it down.
3. Now that you have identified the emotion, close your eyes (only if safe to do) and imagine putting that emotion 5 feet in front of you.
4. Give it a form. With your eyes closed, give your emotion a size, shape, even a color.

5. Now that it has a form, e.g., shape color etc., watch it for a few moments and recognize it for what it is.
6. When you're ready, let the emotion return to you. Does it feel the same? What's different about it?

Once you've completed this exercise, take a moment to reflect on what you noticed about your experience. Did you notice any change in the emotion when you got a little distance from it? What about changes in your reactions to the emotion? What size, shape, and color did you give the emotion? Did the emotion feel different in some way once the exercise was finished?

As stated earlier, learning to identify various emotions takes time. However, it will be well worth the time.

2

Do a Self-Evaluation

What are your strengths? What are your weaknesses? I actually don't like the word "weakness" – because it feels so negative. So I use the word "struggle" instead. Moving forward, when the word "weakness" appear, mentally, substitute "struggle". It means "the things you are not naturally as great at."

Are you willing to accept that you're not perfect and that you could work on some areas to make yourself a better person? Have the courage to look at yourself honestly – it can change your life.

Throughout life, we acquire abilities and skills that help us to compete with others or to reach our goals. We also have underdeveloped areas of struggles that need improvement, identifying them can help you stabilize your personal life and nurture your professional interactions.

I didn't want to list this as the very first way to improve your emotional intelligence. Why? Because, one of the hardest things to do in life is to be completely honest with yourself about yourself. It requires total truthfulness about strengths and struggles regardless of how those revelations make us feel about ourselves. If it had been listed first, it may have discouraged you from going any further.

Tips & Exercises

One of the easiest and quickest ways is to take one of the many strength and weakness test that are available – either the pencil and paper type or on-line. Probing your own strengths and struggles will clarify what's the best next step is and how you can improve yourself. It will also tell you more on where you would like to focus and where you would be able to improve yourself most.

If you want to really recognize your strengths, you need other people to hold up a mirror. When you see your reflection through the eyes of those who know you, you can begin to identify your most unique talents. When it comes to assessing our own talents, we're full of blind spots. If you can see yourself through the eyes of others, your vision will become less blurry.

Another approach is to create a personal SWOT analysis. For those of you not familiar with a SWOT analysis, briefly, a SWOT analysis is an analytical method, which is used to identify and categories significant internal factors (i.e. Strengths and Weaknesses) and external factors (i.e. Opportunities and Threats) an organization faces. This approach can be applied to your emotional intelligence as well.

Stop! Before you start investing the time in doing this analysis first be sure you are ready to be honest with yourself, truly honest. When looking at an organization, it's easy to identify what's wrong with the company, the job, the boss and the co-workers. Now, it's time to look inside and identify and accept our strengths and struggles. No one is perfect, we all have things we are great or pretty terrible at. This tool is for you, so be honest. What is the worst that can happen? You make positive changes that lead to a new opportunity?

To get started, you need to revisit or take an EI assessment. Then, create a SWOT Analysis form by dividing a sheet of paper into four equal sections. Label the upper left section "Strengths", the upper right section "Weakness", bottom left "Opportunities, and the bottom right section "Threats". You can also find examples of the format online.

From the EI assessment, regardless of the score, but based on how you see yourself, decide which of the four categories to list the item, i.e. Empathy. Based on how you see yourself, you might list it under "Opportunities" or "Strengths". Do the same for the remainder of the items/areas revealed on your assessment.

Then reflect on feedback that you've gotten from close friends, loved ones, co-workers, your boss and others. They will serve as indicators as to whether they are candidates for improvements or currently serve you well where they are. Remember, no one source or assessment will provide you with all of the information you need. Each is like a piece to a jig saw puzzle.

With both your strengths and your struggles, it is important to always evolve. Be open to new experiences and things that will change you. As you grow in your career and life in general, you will change. Your strengths and weaknesses will change. Be flexible and open to new experiences. Consider assessing them every 3 to 5 years.

3

Pay Attention to your Behavior and Feelings

Notice how you act when you're experiencing certain emotions, and how that affects your day-to-day life. Does it impact your communication with others, your productivity, or your overall sense of well-b4eing? It all starts with you. Once you start accepting responsibility for how you feel and how you behave, this will have a positive impact on all areas of your life.

We pay attention to our feelings as a way of increasing our self-awareness – the key to emotional intelligence. Our feelings are *always with* us, whether we want them to or not, ***and,*** whether we acknowledge them or not; so we don't have a choice about their existence.

Be Observant. Pay attentions to emotions. Emotions contain valuable information about other people, relationships and our surroundings. The better you are at reading and understanding emotions, the more appropriately you will be able to respond.

The type, frequency, and intensity of emotions can have a profound effect on the depth and breadth of our personal and professional relationships. The emotions that people witness in others may (and usually do) influence their current as well as future relationships with that person.

Many people are disconnected from their emotions—especially strong ones such as anger, sadness, fear, and joy. This may be the result of negative childhood experiences that taught you to try to shut off your feelings. But although we can distort, deny, or numb our feelings, we can't eliminate them. They're still there, whether we're aware of them or not. Acknowledge your emotion and then determine its source – is it based on a bad experience or a past interaction that may be influencing the current situation?

Feelings are an important part of you. In order to live fully and effectively, you need many sources of information (e.g., your senses, your thoughts, your perceptions) to guide you, motivate you, and help you make sense of things. Your emotions provide one such source. When you are feeling something consider asking yourself the following kinds of questions:

- What is this feeling?
- What is this feeling telling me about this situation?
- Why has this feeling come up right now?

For example, say you're at work and someone over talks you during a meeting – not allowing you to finish your sentence. What emotions arise when this happens? On the other hand, how do you feel when you get praised for good work? Getting into the practice of naming your emotions as sadness, embarrassment, joy, contentment, or any other number of feelings is an important skill.

If you find it difficult to notice or name what you are feeling, it may require that you pay attention to your body. Most feelings are experienced in the body. For example:

- Fear may show up as an upset stomach, diarrhea stomach or a dry or "cracked" feeling in your throat.

- Feeling embarrassed or insecure might cause you to withdraw from conversations and disconnect.

- Feeling overwhelmed might cause you to panic and lose track of what you were doing, or cry.

Feelings are also connected to your behavior. If you aren't sure of how you feel, but you realize that you are acting in a way that sends a clear message to others, you may be able to **infer** what you are feeling from your behavior. For example, if you have an angry facial expression (frown or furrowed brow) or harsh tone of voice when you are talking with a friend or co-worker, it may be that you are angry or frustrated with that person without recognizing it.

Get used to interpreting body language as a means to understand an individual's complete communication. With practice, you will get better.

Tips & Exercises

Here are some useful questions to consider when deciding how to respond to your feelings:

- Does the intensity of my feelings match the situation?
- What are my options for expressing my feelings?
- What are the consequences of each option for me/others?

- Even doing something like taking a deep breath or going for a walk to think about it can be a way of responding to your feelings. Remember that you have many options when it comes to expressing emotions.
- Practice deciding how to behave. You can't help what emotions you feel, but you can decide how you want to respond to them.
- Being able to quickly calm yourself down and relieve stress helps you stay balanced, focused, and in control.
- Being able to connect to your emotions—having a moment-to-moment awareness of your emotions and how they influence your thoughts and actions—is the key to understanding yourself and remaining calm and focused in tense situations with others.

Learning to experience your feelings fully and expressing them in ways that are adaptive and healthy is not a simple process, but there are some key components that can help. In general, it is important to become a good observer of your feelings, to accept and value them, and to attend to what they signal to you.

4

Manage your Thoughts

Ever hear the song or phrase "What you see is what you get"? It's also true that what you think is what you get. Thoughts lead to feeling. Your thoughts lead directly to your feelings, so if you are feeling bad, you most likely have a negative thought that is making you feel that way.

Studies tell us that we produce up to 50,000 thoughts a day and 70% to 80% of those are negative. This translates into 40,000 negative thoughts a day that need managing. That's a pretty tall order. Where do we start? We start with Thought Awareness.

Thought Awareness is the process by which you observe your thoughts and become aware of what is going through your head. Thought awareness is the first step in the process of managing negative thoughts, as you can only manage thoughts that you're aware of. Thought Awareness helps you identify the negative thinking, unpleasant memories, and misinterpretation of situations that may interfere with your performance and damage your self-confidence. This allows you to deal with them.

Some of us pay much more attention to negatives than to positives. Sometimes this negative thinking ("stinking thinking") becomes automatic and takes on a life of its own. Counter with Positive Thinking.

Tips & Exercises

Change the Channel. Just like watching your TV, if you don't like what's on, you change the channel to something you prefer. Do the same with your thoughts. You can do something else - call a friend, watch a movie, go for a walk, a run... there are so many things you can do. Here you want to select an activity that you can do straight away, once the negative thought comes in.

Stop It! You are the boss, so as simple as this sounds, the first thing you can do is to send a command to yourself, say "Stop It"! A direct command, given with a firm order tone, will interrupt the behavior, like stopping you in your track.

A good example of this, done in a humorous way, is a great Mad TV sketch on YouTube starring Bob Newhart as - what else - a psychiatrist. His patient tells him she has a pathological fear of being buried alive in a box. He has two words of wisdom: "Stop it!"

Shocked and somewhat taken aback, she goes on to detail her other issues: she's bulimic, she's been stuck in a series of abusive relationships, and she's a compulsive hand-washer. "Stop it," he says. "Just stop it, what are you, some kind of nut?"
"

After five minutes of this, she's had it. Outraged, she protests that she hates this therapy, it's moving too fast, it's ridiculously simplistic. "You want more?" asks Newhart. She nods. He leans across his desk. "Stop it or I'll bury you alive in a box!" he shouts.

A truly funny skit. But what about that idea that we could just "stop it" - stop our thoughts, fears, destructive behaviors? It's not that easy, right? Right?

In order to stop it, we've got to be aware of the pattern in the first place. We've got to want to stop it. You can develop the ability to create new thoughts and to debunk untrue thoughts and beliefs. Like any change of habits, it takes time – so set aside time to establish a new pattern. Then practice, practice, practice!

If you start thinking of other possible ways of looking at the situation, you will begin to feel better immediately. What you focus on expands!

5

Practice Being in the Present

"I never think of the future. It comes soon enough."
- Albert Einstein -

We spend a great deal of time focusing on the past or future. However we spend very little time on the present. Try focusing on the present – see what you discover. Start by noticing what you're feeling, right now. Observe without judgment (evaluating feelings as "good" "bad" "right" "wrong) or trying to 'fix' anything; just notice your emotions a few times per day.

As humans we tend to spend a lot of time in the past or the future. Our brains race from one thought to another, and if you analyze them very carefully, only a few of them are actually focused on the present moment. Most of them have either a step in the past or the future. We spend much time thinking about what was and what could have been. And we spend an equal if not more time projecting into the future and wondering about what may happen.

We need to live more in the moment. Living in the moment—also called mindfulness—is a state of active, open, intentional attention on the present. It has been said that Mindfulness reduces stress, boosts immune functioning, reduces chronic pain, lowers blood pressure, and helps patients cope with cancer. Mindful people are happier, more exuberant, more empathetic, and more secure. They have higher self-esteem and are more accepting of their own weaknesses. Being present has other benefits. You'll feel fewer negative emotions and more positive emotions. Guilt and regret comes from focusing on the past. Fear and stress on the other hand comes from focusing on the future. A focus on the present fosters openness, equanimity, and gratitude.

The following exercises and activities will help us be more in the present.

Tips & Exercises

1. **Focus on what's right in front of you.** Or around you. Use your senses. Just look at what's right in front of you right now. Take a walk and listen to the sounds around you, i.e., birds, airplanes, traffic, people talking. Feel the fabric of your clothes and focus on how they feel.

2. **Focus on your breathing** - Find a quiet place such as your office (with the door closed), your bedroom just before going to bed focus your mind on your inhaling and exhaling. Can you hear the breath come in and out? Can you feel your lungs expand and contract? What about your chest? Watch the natural changes in your breathing as you become more relaxed. You might notice that your breath starts shallow and fast, but becomes deeper and more regular as you relax.

3. **Focus on your inner body** - This is a bit similar to focusing on your breathing. In both examples you focus on what's inside you rather than the outside. I guess you

could say it is energy inside of your body. How your body feels from the inside. Close your eyes, see if you can feel the energy in your body. Don't feel defeated if you can't as this takes lots of practice.

4. **Do one thing at a time** - Do one thing at a time and do it with full dedication as if it's the only thing that exists in the whole universe. Don't mix two or more activities together. You will end up doing nothing perfectly. Our mind has been conditioned to think about our past and future all the time. That's why it needs a lot of practice to break this habit, and start living in the present moment. You can start this practice by doing one thing at a time. When walking just walk. When listening just listen. When eating just eat. Do one thing at a time - the essence of mindfulness acting with undivided attention.

Practice "letting go". Permit the past to pass. Make a mental note of the emotions or feelings you experienced and the situations that led up to them but stay in the present, even as you see things you wish you could change.

Begin each day with the intention of making the best and most of it. It may not always go as planned, but it can go more smoothly if you put it in perspective. Part of living a well-balanced life is learning how to deal with adversity, unforeseen events and uncertainty. If you practice not letting things get to you, you will not only learn to live a well-balanced and less stressful life, you will learn to live in and savor the moment. Once you've done everything you can within your control, let your life unfold. Be prepared for the future, but don't worry about it.

While we can't anticipate and plan for everything in our lives, we can decide how, where and when to concentrate our energies. This may require some critical thinking and problem solving, but in the end it will lead to much less stress and a well-balanced life.

You won't be good at it at first, most likely. Your mind will wander. Don't beat yourself up about that. Don't get discouraged. Just practice. Every opportunity you get, practice. Don't resist the present; embrace it. As each moment reveals itself to you, greet it with unhurried appreciation.

6

Take Responsibility for your Actions

Who is in control of you? The answer of course is – you! If you aren't in control then it's not your fault... right? To change what's wrong in your life, you must believe *and* accept that you're the one in control.

If you hurt someone's feelings, apologize directly – don't ignore what you did or avoid the person. People are usually more willing to forgive and let bygones be bygones if you make an honest attempt to make things right. Don't make an excuse.

Try this, the next time you catch yourself in the middle of an excuse, change your words. Instead, admit *why* you really didn't get that thing done. Were you too lazy, too tired, or just feeling like doing something else? It's okay to admit it. In fact, it's best to admit your real reasons for not doing something before you move on. If you never admit to something you did wrong, then how can you learn from it? One of the key parts of accepting responsibility is being able to say, "I really messed up. I won't do it again."

Another way to accept responsibility is to stop putting the blame on others. Blaming other people instead of yourself will not only make you vindictive. It will make you powerless to change your life for the better.

Tips & Exercises

Here's a sure fire approach that works - affirm. Say "I am responsible!" Say it several times until it feels completely true. When you create affirmations, you need to focus on what you want, not on what you don't want. Practice saying your affirmations for 30 minutes a day. Say them in your head and out loud, even if it's uncomfortable to do at first. Affirmations can be a powerful tool to help you manage your emotions.

Affirmations work in the same manner like computer commands. If we put garbage in a computer we get garbage as output. (Hence the phrase GIGO which means Garbage In, Garbage Out). Affirmations program the mind, which then affects one's life, and even the events and circumstances one goes through.

It is very important to choose only positive affirmations. Here are a few to get you started:

- I am healthy and happy.
- I have a lot of energy.
- My mind is calm.
- I am calm and relaxed in every situation.
- My thoughts are under my control.
- I have a wonderful and satisfying job.
- I am successful in whatever I do.
- Everything is getting better every day.

Sometime affirmations work fast, but more often they need time to make changes. So don't be discouraged when change doesn't happen overnight – after all we didn't become who we are overnight.

7

Practice Humility

You are secure in your self-regard. You know your capabilities and strengths, and you can be quietly confident about it. Give others a chance to shine – put the focus on them, and don't worry too much about getting praise for yourself.

There are several definitions for humility. The one that I like most is "humility as modesty, lacking pretense, not believing that you are superior to others".

Humility is often confused with timidity. Humility has nothing to do with being meek, weak, or indecisive. Humility is all about maintaining our pride about who we are, about our achievements, about our worth – but without arrogance.

Tips & Exercises

Here are a few suggestions on practicing humility:

1. At the top of the list are these three words that are guaranteed to win friends and build relationships; "You are right."

2. Seek others' input on how you are showing up in your personal as well as professional relationships; how you're performing as a team member. Ask: "How am I doing?" It takes humility and courage to ask such a question. And even more of both to consider the answer.

3. Share the stage. In today's environment, few people accomplish things alone. That being said, you should always look for the opportunity to acknowledge others, regardless to how large or small their contribution may have been. It doesn't hurt to share the credit. You will gain more by sharing the pie than by eating it all yourself – regardless to how to good it taste.

There are many benefits to practicing humility. First and perhaps foremost - it reduces anxiety. It also improves relationships and encourages more openness. Paradoxically, it enhances one's self-confidence. When you practice humility, you gain the respect of others.

People who practice humility tend to reflect inward, but when it comes to where they focus their energy, it's all about other people. In addition to being concerned for others, people who exude humility also act on their compassion. According to a 2012 study, humble people are more likely than prideful people to help out a friend. Additionally, research also shows that humble people show a more charitable and generous nature toward other people.

"A great man is always willing to be little."
— Ralph Waldo Emerson

8

Listen to Understand, Not to Respond

Often while listening to someone, we are formulating replies in our mind, waiting for a lull in the conversation so we can interject. Try instead to just listen. Suspend all judgment and give the person your undivided attention.

Be quiet. Mentally eliminate other noises and distractions. Being quiet gives you the opportunity to hear the words, the tone, and the meaning behind the words. It gives you the chance to *observe the speaker's body language*. When communicating with another individual. Instead of rehearsing your response while the other person is speaking, focus your mind and attention on asking questions to clarify and understanding what the person is saying.

Ask questions to ensure that you understand. Just because you heard the words and observed the body language, don't assume that you understand. If a particular point is unclear to you, ask a question to clarify it before you respond. Asking questions shows the speaker that you're interested in what's being said. It enhances your relationship.

Effective listening involves observing body language and noticing inconsistencies between verbal and non-verbal messages. Here are 3 sure fire ways to improve your listening skills.

Tips & Exercises

1. **Remove Distractions** - Focus on what is being said. Don't check messages on your cell phones, don't doodle, shuffle papers, look out the window, and or multitask. Avoid unnecessary interruptions. These behaviors disrupt the listening process

and send messages to the speaker that you are disinterested or distracted.

2. **Avoid Personal Bias –** We all have a bias or two. Some of us like spicy foods, some of do not. Being impartial isn't easy as we all have a POV (point of view) – even things we know very little about. Don't become irritated and don't let the person's speaking style or mannerisms distract you from what they are really saying. Everybody has a different way of speaking - some people are for example more nervous or shy than others, some have regional accents or make excessive hand movements, some people like to pace back and forth as they talk - others like to stand behind a lectern. Focus on what is being said - try to ignore "environmental noise" and styles of delivery.

3. **Don't Interrupt**. Be professional. It's rude to interrupt someone while they're talking, because it shows that you aren't really listening - you're too eager to make sure your own two cents are heard. If you tend to jump in with your opinion before the other person has finished speaking, make a point of quitting your habit of interrupting. Be patient, wait until a

person has finished his or her thought before you speak. If you do interrupt, it's a good idea to apologize and ask the person to please continue what he or she was saying.

To enhance your listening skills, you need to let the other person know that you are listening to what he or she is saying. Start using active listening today to become a better communicator, improve your workplace productivity, and develop better relationships.

One More Exercise

Listening skills are central to the emotionally competent leader. However, the skill of listening requires far more than technique. True listening requires a mindset that includes the following elements:

- a respectful attitude toward the speaker even when the content of the speaker's message is abrasive
- a open mind willing to hear and seek understanding of the messages of the speaker
- placing the speaker as a human equal thus worthy of the listener's attention

These qualities are far beyond technique. Therefore, although the how to's of listening can be taught, unless the mindset is established first, the listening will seem fake or phony. Leaders must examine not only their technique, but also their hearts to truly impact their ability to listen.

Also, listening is far easier when the speaker and the listener have similar values about a particular topic. The most challenging listening occurs when the speaker is saying something in direct opposition to the listener's point of view, in these moments, the emotionally competent leader is able to maintain genuine listening and practice self-control, thus ensuring that the speaker is heard.

The intent of this exercise is to practice both technique and mindset. By developing the skill and mindset, you will forge greater bonds and a more open workplace atmosphere. This exercise is also to remind you of the importance of developing good listening habits and to practice listening in situations that are challenging.

Directions: Part 1

1. Select a partner
2. One person will be the speaker, the other assumes the role of listener
3. The speaker should choose a subject that he/she feels ***very*** strongly about
4. The listener should use listening skills that include asking clarifying questions, reflecting both feeling and content of the speaker's message, and practicing appropriate non-verbal's. Under no circumstances should you, the listener, add your comments or evaluative remarks during the exercise.
5. Switch roles after 7 minutes.

9

Walk in the Other Person's Shoes

Easy said but not easy done. To walk in someone else shoes, you must first *take yours off*. Increasing your ability to empathize can help you get closer to others, win their support when you need it, and defuse potentially high-charged situations. By showing another person that you really understand where he's coming from, you establish a certain level of connection.

Try seeing it from their point of view. Empathy is an extremely powerful emotion. Increasing your ability to empathize can help you get closer to others, win their support when you need it, and defuse potentially high-charged situations.

The ability to empathize with others is relative to a person's capacity to identify, feel and understand his own feelings and thereby being able to project one's feelings onto others. By showing another person that you really understand where he's coming from, you gain a certain level of respect. You demonstrate, for example, that you're not self-centered.

You need to put yourself in the other person's shoes and feel his pain, joy, hopes, or fears. Think about how you would feel if you were in their situation. Actively imagine how it must be to go through the experiences they're having and what might alleviate some of their hardship in terms of support and care. When you see someone experience a strong emotion, ask yourself, "How would I react in the same situation?"

Tips & Exercises

Listening is the key. Focus solely on listening to the other person. Strive to quiet the internal talk. Remember, you don't have to agree with what is said. Your goal is simply to listen, acknowledge and strive to understand the other person's point of view.

Learn to listen for feelings. People don't always express their true feelings or concerns directly, so listen for words that express feelings and needs. Keep in mind as you listen that all of us want to be recognized and included in the process.

Make time for people. As busy and pressed for time as you might be, you must still make addressing the concerns and feelings of others a top priority. If you don't, you send the message that you consider others and their issues unimportant. Remember, actions speak louder than words.

Acknowledge (and mean it). Use the effective technique of paraphrasing to play back what you heard someone say. It's a good way to check for accuracy and understanding. Also, be sure to clarify the emotions you think you "heard" in spoken words or "saw" in body language. For example, you might say something like "sounds like you are feeling frustrated about this project." Or, "looks like you're happy about this assignment."

Don't judge. When you're tempted to criticize or dismiss the opinions or feelings of others, don't. Resist the impulse to speak. Think on an emotional level, as well as a cognitive level, about what others may be experiencing. Also, consider the merits of their point of view before you respond. Always try to make your responses objective—and non-judgmental.

In closing, this "Tips and Exercise", let me point out that empathy is, luckily, a learned skill that we can develop and grow through consistent practice. Therefore, if you are willing to increase your understanding of the behavior of others, it is never too late to learn it.

10

Practice Social Responsibility (SR)

Today there is a growing desire, even demand for more social responsibility in the workplace, especially from employees and customers. Studies are documenting that social responsibility is a recruitment and retention advantage, particularly among the younger generations. Workers reward socially responsible organizations with increased engagement, which leads to increased productivity and revenue.

But it doesn't stop there. More and more social responsibility is needed at the individual level. While not fully recognized by most, it is a key area of emotional intelligence. Social responsibility is one of the highest levels of emotional experience. It demonstrates that you really care about others, especially those less fortunate. Being socially responsible isn't about personal gain — it's about what you can contribute to help other people.

SR means doing your part to help the environment, volunteering your time to those in need, mentoring our youth, and being conscientious and courteous in all you do.

- SR means to be internally motivated to act compassionately.
- Being socially responsible isn't about personal gain — it's about what you can contribute to help other people. Be it a community organization, team member, a co-worker with too much on their plate. Pitch in – help out.
- SR is promoting a proactive stance towards positively influencing and affecting the people and environments around you.

Social responsibility can take many forms. Consider the following: Years ago when my son was young, I asked a friend of mine if he would tutor my son in math. He agreed that he would. We determined the cost but instead of me paying him, he asked me if I could pay the charity of his choice.

Reflect on how you spent your time last week. What activities and tasks did you spend your time on?

Tips & Exercises

- You may just start off volunteering once a month somewhere that suits your skills, abilities or interests.
- If you have the choice of two products and one product supports a good cause or was produced in a more ethical way, then purchase that product.
- In the workplace, look for opportunities to contribute to your team or work group. If you notice that a team member or a co-worker seems to be behind in their work or appear to be over loaded, rather than say, "That's not my job". Instead, say, "Can I help" or "Is there anything I can help you with"?
- You're at home watching your favorite TV show, your wife is making dinner. Do you continue watching the show and let her continue with dinner preparation or do

you ask, "Can I help?" or perhaps offer your assistance without asking?

Only through a commitment to embrace and embed social responsibility into your personal value and belief system can you truly become socially responsible in all you do.

A final thought on how to think of social responsibility is: "Be a part of the solution, not a part of the problem".

11

Practice Emotional Flexibility

Emotional Flexibility is the ability to respond flexibly to changing emotional circumstances. Everyone has set ways of doing things. For an organization – even an individual to be more efficient, it needs a certain amount of rules and regulations to operate within. However, you can experience problems when you get stuck in a rut and become inflexible to change.

Being emotionally intelligent involves knowing when to stick to and when to switch your emotional attachments. When it's time to move on, people high in emotional intelligence can make that adjustment.

Although you might find it uncomfortable to try new things, remember, *no pain, no gain.* Part of growing as a person involves learning new skills and approaches and experiencing new relationships and places.

Generally when we think of flexibility, we think of something that is achieved on the physical level alone - such as stretching before working out or the person that can bend over backwards and do a hand stand. There is something, however, to be said about living a 'flexible' life. That is, being mentally and emotionally flexible. And, there's one really important thing to know about Flexibility. Changing your mind, or adjusting your approach, is not weak or a sign of lack of competence. It's brave, a sign of strength and self-regard.

Emotional flexibility enables individuals to experience the full range of emotions, like happiness, sadness, or anger, but be able to express them appropriately and then leave that emotional expression behind when it is time to move on. Here are two activities you can try to improve your emotional flexibility: *Cognitive Reappraisal and Adapt to Change.*

Tips & Exercises

Cognitive Reappraisal (how you see an event), sometimes referred to as reframing, is an emotion regulation strategy that involves changing the trajcctory of an emotional response by reinterpreting the meaning of the emotional stimulus. Here's an example.

You take a test and score an 85. Your first reaction may be one of disappointment because you studied hard, stayed up all night. You think you should have done better – perhaps get the top score. However when you reappraise, you began to feel better - perhaps elated, cheerful, overjoyed. Why? Because the subject isn't your favorite; you've only scored in the 70's in the past; this was the last class you needed to graduate.

"The measure of intelligence is the ability to change."
- Albert Einstein -

Adapt to Change. Change is constantly around us. Sometimes it is so minute we don't notice it, while other times it is so severe and sudden that it knocks us off our feet. We should try to make a conscious effort every day to be adaptable to change. While it's not as easy as it sounds, it can be made less difficult by identifying that which needs to be changed in your life by trying to foresee outcomes and considering the future.

The road to Emotional Flexibility starts with Self-Awareness. Self-aware people know themselves. They understand their own strengths and development areas. They observe their behavior and that of others, and can provide an accurate description of their relationship to the environment. Those who are self-aware perceive their behaviors, emotions, thoughts and demonstrate mastery over them.

12

Take Charge of Your Happiness

It's your responsibility. No one else! Happiness comes from the inside out. A person who manages his or her emotions well wakes up happy in the morning. People prefer being around other people who are happy. Happy leaders have followers who are very engaged. Very few people really know how to manage their happiness. People all too often associate happiness with material goods or with getting things from others. The really happy people are the givers. The people who spread happiness tend to be happier themselves.

Research even shows that happy people live longer. Be optimistic. Feel deeply grateful for the things you have. This is a very effective way to be happy. If you feel grateful for the things you have, you not only become happier but it also helps you to bring more into your life. Researchers have found that exercise, healthy diets, and regular sleep are key factors in growing more happy and staying that way.

People will appreciate you more, you can get through tough times easier, you'll feel better, and you'll be more helpful to others. If you have been looking for happiness, the good news is that your choices, thoughts and actions can influence your level of happiness. We all want to be happy. But we have preconceived notions or beliefs about what needs to happen in our lives before we can be happy.

Tips & Exercises

Make happiness a priority. Being confident about who you are is the first step to happiness. If happiness is not at the top of your list then other things will take precedence. If other things take precedence, they may well interfere with your efforts to feel good. Develop happiness routines and make them a part of your everyday living.

Remind yourself however you can to do what you need to do and reward yourself as often as possible for doing what you've done.

Do things that make you happy. Although this sounds obvious, many people simply forget to do things from which they gain pleasure. And do them as often as possible. Don't take life too seriously. Play and have fun. Although we all have responsibilities there's no reason why we can't approach much of our lives in a playful manner. In fact, those who do so will undoubtedly be happier. One of my favorite saying is "let the child out".

Live in the present moment (Mindfulness). The author, Henry Miller once said "Every moment is a golden one for him who has the vision to recognize it as such." The only moment in which we can truly be happy is the present moment. The only moment over which we have control is the present moment. So be happy now! Because if not now, then when?

Carve out some "me time" every day. Even if your day is super-packed, make some time for yourself. Whether you're reading a great book during your lunch break, watching your favorite show before you go to bed, or waking up early enough to mediate, making that time for yourself can help you feel centered. No matter how bad we think our problems are, you can almost guarantee that there's someone out there with much bigger problems than ours.

Practice Optimism. Positive thinking helps us to be healthier, more productive and ultimately happier. Yet for most of us it is hard to practice optimism on a regular basis. Often it's easy to blame oneself, feel sorry, and/or put oneself down. Positive and optimistic people lead themselves by constantly finding encouragement within They surround themselves with other positive people. And they inspire others despite their own personal adversity.

Maintain a positive mental attitude (PMA). Begin each day with the intention of making the best and most of it. It may not always go as planned, but it can go more smoothly if you put it in perspective. Part of living a well-balanced life is learning how to deal with adversity, unforeseen events and uncertainty. If you practice not letting things get to you, you will not only learn to live a well-balanced and less stressful life, you will learn to live in and savor the moment.

People are not happy all the time. Everyone has times when they feel sad, frustrated, guilty, angry, and so on. People that demonstrate a high degree of happiness are just more resilient and better at maintaining a state of happiness for a longer period or when called for. We may all feel negative at times, but try to bounce back and live in the moment, and be content with everything you do.

13

Be Compassionate

Compassion is defined as the emotion that one feels in response to the suffering of others that motivates a desire to help. In fact, research shows that the one giving the gift usually feels a larger pulse of dopamine (the neurotransmitter responsible for feeling happiness) than the person receiving the gift.

Why develop compassion? This question is often asked when we don't fully understand compassion. Because compassion is generally associated with unpleasant feeling or emotions, we often try to avoid it rather than understand it and process the ensuing emotion. True compassion is hard work, but it's worthwhile.

Put yourself in situation of the other party mentally. Suffering is universal. Almost all of us have felt joy and pain. The particular details may be unique, but the themes are universal. So, remind yourself of a time when you went through something related.

Tips & Exercises

Try this. Imagine that a loved one is suffering. Something terrible has happened. The more severe, the more vivid the imagination will be, i.e., a broken arm, leg or a death in the family. Now try to imagine the pain they are going through. Imagine the suffering in as much detail as possible. After doing this practice for a couple of weeks, you should try moving on to imagining the suffering of others you know, not just those who are close to you. This means that you should experience the other persons suffering or emotions from that person's frame of reference – walking in their shoes.

Here's a short story I came across on compassion. After reading it, reflect on the emotions you experience.

"When my husband of 28 years died eighteen months ago, I felt there was nothing left to live for. I was on the brink of ending it all when my doctor, whom I had know for a long time, put me in touch with support group. I met several women there – one that befriended me. We go out together, laugh together, even cry together sometimes. During tough times and when things are really bad, we talk and she knows how I feel.

Remember, it does not take anything big to show compassion to others; sometimes, just a few small deeds can bring a smile to someone's face. As a matter of fact smiling is contagious. Therefore

1. Smile more. Nothing warms a person more than receiving a smile. They will almost always return the smile. Usually whatever they were feeling is lessened
2. Help or serve others. Recently I've volunteered to be a table host and server at a facility that feeds the homeless, poor, or those that just need a meal. I find that in addition to a meal, the guests really enjoy being respected and treated with dignity.
3. Other examples include:

    - Hold the door open for the person behind you.

- Give someone your parking spot.
- Ask someone how they are doing, and stop to listen to the answer.

As you can see, acts of compassion need not be something large, though it can be. An act of compassion is a selfless act by one person to show kindness and benefit another.

This quote by the Dalai Lama says it all.

If you want others to be happy, practice compassion. If you want to be happy, practice compassion.

14

Build a Good Relationship with Yourself

This doesn't mean becoming a narcissist. It does mean however, that you should have a "healthy" opinion of who you are, your strengths and challenges. Areas where you excel as well as areas where you struggle should also be identified.

Maintaining a good relationship with yourself is no different than maintaining a good relationship with a partner, a friend, or a family member. All relationships take time, effort, and good communication. Having a good relationship with yourself improves your relationships with others. If we are not connected and emotionally available to ourselves, we cannot be connected and emotionally available for others. We all know this. But knowing it and actualizing it are two different things.

So what does a healthy relationship with yourself look like? Here are some tips and exercises that will get you started.

Tips & Exercises

Care for your needs. Cultivating a healthy relationship with yourself is by caring for your basic physical needs. That includes getting enough sleep and rest, eating nutritious meals and exercising.

Know thy self-better. Another way to get to know yourself better is to spend quality time with yourself. Drop everything that you're doing and spend a few minutes with yourself. This concept is known as self-observation. By spending a few quiet moments with yourself, you can begin to assess your behaviors, your thought process, and determine the endless possibilities of your personal growth. This will lead to a better understanding of yourself and allow you to perform better self-care.

Self-Talk - We talk to ourselves all day, every day. What are you saying to yourself? When do you talk to yourself most? What percentage of your self-talk is positive/negative? When are you most negative/positive? Learn to replace negative talk with positive talk. Positive thinking doesn't mean that you keep your head in the sand and ignore life's less pleasant situations. Positive thinking just means that you approach unpleasantness in a more positive and productive way. You think the best is going to happen, not the worst.

Other tips for taking care of self:

- Love yourself unconditionally without being self-righteous or arrogant.
- Don't abuse yourself with tobacco, coffee, drugs, alcohol, or other substances.
- Replace negative thoughts and judgments with positive supportive ones.
- Let go of blame if you have been hurt in the past; become empowered.
- Take care of your physical health through exercise, proper nutrition, and rest.
- Don't give up when things go wrong. Make a commitment to the relationship you have with yourself.

- Treat yourself (and others) with respect, kindness, and compassion.
- Acknowledge that everyone fallible (including you), but capable of improvement and growth.
- Challenge unhealthy perceptions of yourself. Consider new ways of looking at yourself, others, and your relationships.

Last but perhaps the most important of all - understanding that a good relationship with yourself takes work and time commitment. It's crucial to have a great relationship with ourselves because it's the only relationship that you are guaranteed to have every day of your life!

15

Take Time to Reflect

To engage with emotions challenges requires inner work--personal reflection time. Time alone gives you time to reflect about your feelings and emotions so that you can better understand them. Allows you to sort out and clarify your thoughts and emotions. Life can be overwhelming. When we use reflection as a tool, we're able to stand back objectively and take a look at our lives and what we deal with. It is also the ability to reflect on the "here and now", on your feelings and thoughts. This also includes reflecting on the thoughts, emotions and the feelings of others. Reflection also helps us learn more about ourselves so that we go on to make better choices.

Without ever reflecting, we're more likely to focus on how much we've failed at, rather than see how much we've been successful at. At the end of each day, set aside 30 minutes to reflect on the different emotions you experienced during the day. Write them down. Now comes the hard part. Reflect on what generated the emotion. What behavior followed it? Was it appropriate? How can you respond more effectively the next time?

Tips & Exercises

Exercise. A favorite times to reflect (other than at the end of the day or while driving) is during one of my walks or workouts at the gym. I like to take that time to think about my life, and my work. Some of my best ideas come during "gym time". If you don't do the gym, run or have some other form of daily exercise, consider just taking a walk and using that time for reflection.

Journaling. Journaling is an insightful way to record your thoughts while they are happening. Writing your thoughts down lets you deal with issues as they arise. But the main advantage is that it gives you a time to reflect. Self-reflection is the key to changing how you feel and how you cope. Physically writing things out forces you to focus on what is important.

Writing can be done daily or only when you feel you need to express yourself. Most people like to set aside a fixed time of day, such as before getting ready for bed. It really doesn't matter when you do it. As Nike says, "Just do it". There is no right or wrong way. Remember that expressing your emotions in your journal can be a great outlet for stress relief, so try to write about your thoughts, hopes, fears, frustrations, and any other emotions you are experiencing.

Here's a suggestions for dealing with frustration. **Stop and evaluate** – One of the best things you can do is mentally stop yourself, and reflect on the situation. Ask yourself why you feel frustrated. Write it down, and be specific. Then think of one positive thing about your current situation. For instance, if your boss is late for your meeting, then you have more time to prepare. Or, you could use this time to relax a little.

Other ways to reflect. Always set aside time for yourself on a daily basis, even if it is just a few minutes each day. I call it "Me Time". It's time to yourself and it allows you to relax, reflect, or work on a personal hobby that you enjoy.

Here are a few more suggestions:

- Draw or paint – you don't have to be a Michelangelo. You do it to relax.
- Write – We all have a story to tell.
- Reflect on a great moment you recently experienced and why it made you feel good.
- A cup of tea outside or in your bed can be very relaxing
- Read a book that fascinates you – the one you've been putting off
- Take a walk, stretch.

The more you reflect the better you will get at it.

16

Be more Empathetic

Empathy is the ability to notice and understand how another person is feeling and then respond in an appropriate way. It also means appreciating and accepting differences between people, accepting that we have different priorities and capabilities around emotion.

Listening isn't (necessarily) agreeing!

When you use empathy with skill, you show others not just that you are interested in them, but that you respect and value them as well. Empathy is a powerful skill and one of the cornerstones of Emotional Intelligence.

Empathy is a core component of emotional intelligence, and a known contributor to effective interpersonal relations and communication.

The first way to develop this skill is to stop to recognize what it is the other person is feeling? Pay careful attention to their verbal cues and their body language. What do they tell you the person is feeling? Listen to the words that they use, especially the emotionally charged words. What do those words indicate that they are feeling?

Tips & Exercises

To become more empathetic... Try these three steps

Step 1: Imagine Yourself in Their Position
Once you recognize what the other person feels, empathy requires that you feel what are they are feeling. That means you need to put yourself in their position. But it doesn't mean you put yourself in their position in the logical sense of the word. It isn't the ability to say: "Yes, I can imagine how you feel." Instead, it is the ability to say: "Yes, I feel what you are feeling." To develop this skill,

literally imagine yourself in the client's position. Imagine how you would feel.

Step 2: Listen and Accept Their Interpretation

To truly exercise your empathy and your emotional intelligence, you have to be to listen without immediately passing judgment on the facts or the meaning of what is being said. You have to accept their interpretation as being valid and worthwhile.

Step 3: Pause

Before you can manage the emotions of others, you have to be able to manage your own emotions. This means being aware of your emotions. Use pause to decide how your response will help or hurt your achieving the outcome that you need.

"No one cares how much you know, until they know how much you care"

– Theodore Roosevelt

17

Pause...

The ability to pause before reacting is a key component of emotional intelligence. Most of the time, we are on auto pilot. Consider this example.

You spent the last three weeks putting together a report for your boss. You have it sitting on your desk. About 10 minutes before you are to put it in your boss's hand, your co –workers stops by your desk with a cup of coffee for a quick chat. He sits the coffee down next to the report. When he picks it up, it spills on the report. Full of anger, you tell your co-worker off. A few minutes later, you wish you could unsay your angry words. This happens when we are angered or feel threatened and the result is what is commonly known as “blowing a fuse.”— We act quickly before we think.

We get tunnel vision and don’t consider other alternatives other than the perspective that has made us so angry or upset or afraid. When the emotion goes down, we are then able to think more clearly because the logical part of our brain is engaged again.

Most of the time acting immediately is not necessary and not advisable. When we can pause between the feelings we have and the action we want to take, we can usually make a better decision based on both logic and emotion.

When we are in its grip, our impulses override our rationality and we do or say things that we later regret. We are on auto pilot. We can experience a range of reactions from outright anger to ruminating over an event and shutting down or withdrawing – not wanting to play anymore.

The ability to pause before reacting is a key component of emotional and social intelligence. Emotions give us important information. Being completely logical leaves out the information we get from emotions.

Tips & Exercises

Mindfulness is one way to develop the pause between thoughts or feelings and your actions. When you are mindful of an emotion, you step back from the emotion, observe it, and decide if you need or want to act on the emotion and if so in what way you want to act. You remain in control of your actions rather than being at the mercy of your emotions or thoughts.

Mindfulness helps you develop the pause that allows you time to decide if and how you want to act. The more you practice mindfulness, the more likely you can have the pause, even when your emotions are strong.

Take a few deep breaths. Deep breathing delivers more oxygen to the brain and helps us to calm down so that we can focus our attention and think more clearly.

Simply Pause. This is what you want to do when you feel angry: you want to pause, even if just for a couple of seconds, before you say or do anything. When we pause, we are allowing ourselves to respond appropriately to a situation, rather than reacting and doing something that we might regret later.

90 Second Pause. Dr. Jill Bolte Taylor, a Harvard-trained brain scientist discusses the 90 second pause in her insightful book *My Stroke of Insight: A Brain Scientist's Personal Journey*: "Once triggered, the chemical released by my brain surges through my body and I have a physiological experience. Within 90 seconds from the initial trigger, the chemical component of my anger has completely dissipated from my blood and my automatic response is over. If, however, I remain angry after those 90 seconds have passed, then it is because I have chosen to let that circuit continue to run."

Pausing is one of the fundamental anger management strategies. By pausing, you will also gain deeper insight into your emotions, and will be more effective at managing your anger. It has taken us some time to develop our habits and be able to "think on our feet" Except, some time we leave out the thinking part out of the equation and just simply respond or react. Pausing is a cool-down tactics used to prevent emotions from clouding our judgment. You will experience a greater sense of well-being and lower stress levels as you practice this tool.

The right word may be effective, but no word was ever as effective as a rightly timed pause.
- Mark Twain -

18

Develop and Practice Resiliency

We didn't learn our A B C's all at once. We did it a few alphabets at a time. Individuals demonstrate resilience when they can face difficult experiences and rise above them with ease or "roll with the punches". While some research say that we're born with it while others say the opposite. The good news is that emotional resilience is something that can be learned or improved upon no matter what level of it we are born with. Resilient people are able to learn from their mistakes rather than use them as a crutch, see obstacles as challenges to be overcome or adjusted to, and find meaning in difficult situations rather than seeing themselves as a victim of circumstances.

Resilience or the ability to 'bounce back' after encountering problems is an essential trait/skill we all need more of. Psychologists agree that some people seem to be born with more resilience than others. But they also assert that it's possible for all of us to cultivate more of it.

Scientific studies have shown that resilient people show lower levels of depression and are more likely to develop personally as a result of adversity than people with low levels of resilience. Developing resilience is a personal journey. People do not all react the same to traumatic and stressful life events. An approach to building resilience that works for one person might not work for another.

Tips & Exercises

Develop a positive self-image. First and perhaps foremost, develop a positive self-image. Everything starts in the mind – resilient people think well of themselves and see themselves in a positive way. Resilient people take pride in their abilities and what they've done. Recognize your personal strengths.

Develop a Strong Social Network - Having caring, supportive people around you acts as a protective factor during times of crisis. It is important to have people you can trust and confide in. While simply talking about a situation with a friend or loved one will not make troubles go away, it allows you to share your feelings, gain support, receive positive feedback, and come up with possible solutions to problems that just don't seem to go away.

Embrace Change - Flexibility is an essential part of resilience. By learning how to be more adaptable, you'll be better equipped to respond when faced with a life crisis that are inevitable. Resilient people often see these events as an opportunity to branch out in new directions. While some people may be crushed by abrupt changes, highly resilient individuals are able to adapt and thrive.

Be Optimistic - Staying optimistic when things are bleak can be difficult, but maintaining a hopeful outlook is an important part of resiliency. Positive thinking does not mean ignoring the problem in order to focus on positive outcomes. It means understanding that setbacks are transient and that you have the skills and abilities to combat the challenges you face. What you are dealing with may be difficult, but it is important to remain hopeful and positive about a brighter future.

Resilience may take time to build, but so does all things worthwhile. Don't become discouraged if you still struggle many people do. While there may not be any fast or simple solution, you can take steps toward making your situation better and less stressful. Focus on the progress that you have made thus far and planning your next steps, rather than becoming discouraged by the amount of work that still needs to be accomplished. Also, try the following:

- Take care of yourself - Good health — and a regular routine of healthy habits — are foundational to both mental and emotional resilience.
- Mental breaks and relaxation also help keep stress chemicals at bay, reducing the likelihood of feeling, or becoming, overwhelmed and reactive.
- Two other key self-care factors that help nurture resilience: Spending time outdoors and surrounding yourself with people you enjoy.

Finally, take a resilience test to assess whether you should work on improving your coping skills.

"The greatest glory in living lies not in never falling, but in rising every time we fall."
-Nelson Mandela -

19

Express Yourself

Experiencing and expressing emotions are integral parts of life. Rather than ignore or exaggerate your feelings, it is helpful to be able to take your feelings as they are, accept them, think about them, and learn from them. There are times when you are unable to precisely name what you feel. Identifying your feelings may require you to take time to focus on yourself and your feelings in a quiet place.

If you find it difficult to notice or name what you are feeling, it may require that you pay attention to your body. Our bodies are often much smarter than we are. Once you recognize your feelings, you may then more clearly understand and articulate them to your friend or others in a way that is respectful and not hurtful.

It's hard work, but learning to better communicate emotions could impact your physical and psychological health and improve the quality of relationships in your home and work life. Learning how to express feelings without being rude or hurtful therefore is an especially essential skill to develop.

Once you learn how to properly vent these emotions, you'll be able to communicate with others - as well as yourself - much better. It's not always easy to express your feelings, but it's rewarding when you do. Expressing our feelings in an open and nonjudgmental environment leads to bonding and a heightened sense of intimacy - a connection with other people. People, who ignore, dismiss, repress or just ventilate their emotions, are setting themselves up for physical illness.

- Bottled up emotions damage your physical well-being, so learning to express them is important for your physical health as much as for your mental health.

- Holding on to feelings can lead to psychosomatic illnesses like headaches, ulcers, blood pressure, asthma, cardiac problems.
- When you withhold your feelings it can lead to tension in your muscle groups, neck, back, shoulder, and jaws. You can see when someone's angry the tension that builds in their cheek, their neck, even their pelvic area.

Tips & Exercises

Time to Tune in. You need to learn to tune into your body so you understand what it is trying to tell you and how it is reacting to certain circumstances. This means setting aside time to calmly assess and identify what you're feelings and thought patterns.

- In a comfortable space, relax your body for five to ten minutes and do meditation or calming exercises to relax your muscles.
- Ask yourself: "What am I feeling?" and tune into that place in your body that feels emotional sensations like excited, disappointed, anger, etc.
- Calmly listen to what you are feeling, but don't react to it. In this place you are

trying to be an observer rather than an active and reactive participant.

- Practice labeling the emotion that you are actually having. Once you have figured out, somewhat, what you are feeling, ask yourself "where in my body is this feeling?" "What is the shape and texture of this feeling?" "Does this feeling have a color?" Giving concrete form to your feelings helps you accurately and positively express them.
- Talk it out. Talk to yourself as you would a friend; don't use negative associations when thinking about yourself.
- Try writing down a list of emotions, such as anger, delight, sadness, fear, etc. Think about each one and see when or if, you've experienced those emotions. Make a note of how you feel when you are sad, for example (maybe your throat gets choked up and your lips get tight). This will help you identify the emotion when it happens to you.

Identifying and expressing emotions is not a simple process. It takes practice to understand ourselves and to identify how things affect each of us. Sharing feelings effectively often begins with two simple words: "*I feel...*" Fill in the blank then with a single feeling-word such as excited, energized, or confused and you're on your way to expressing your feelings. When you express how you really feel (in an appropriate, non-judgmental manner), problems get solved, relationship issues gct resolved - which leads to a healthier, happier and a more fulfilling life.

20

Sharpen your Reality Testing Skills

Reality Testing – According to MHS (publisher of the EQ-i 2.0), Reality Testing is the "capacity to remain objective by seeing things as they really are. This capacity involves recognizing when emotions or personal bias can cause one to be less objective."

Another definition is Reality Testing is the ability to assess a situation for what it is, rather than the way we wish or fear them to be. Reality testing is the process of checking your personal views against facts, other people's views, and actual events.

Example: “I just said ‘Hi’ to Carol as we pass each other in the hallway. She didn’t answer. She must not like me”.

Reality: There may be other explanations: she didn’t see you; she was deep in thought on an overdue project; she’s worried about her kid that is home sick today.

Another example is, under stress, you might switch your reality testing off, allowing your emotions to cloud your objectivity. Or blow things out of proportion as in the age old saying of “making a mountain out of a molehill”.

Here’s a short story that involves me and my experience with Reality Testing.

Years ago. I was a trainer for a major corporation. Several times a week, my co-workers would stop in and we would all go to lunch. However when the group wanted to go to the Cheesecake Factory, I would not go with them. I would say, “I pass, you go ahead”. This went on for several months. Finally, one day one of them asked “Why don’t you want to go to the Cheesecake Factory?” as they looked at me with a puzzled look on their faces. “I don’t like cheesecake”, I replied. One of them remarked "You do know that they have more than cheesecake at the Cheesecake Factory". All of a sudden, it dawned on me – because I didn't like cheesecake, I didn't see beyond my bias. My realty was that they served cheesecake at the Cheesecake Factory. After that, I did go to the Cheesecake Factory with them and had food other than cheesecake. I still don't go that often but I am aware that they have more than cheesecake there.

This happens too many of us. What's your "cheesecake story"? Why is reality testing important?

Your ability to size up the immediate situation means your emotional responses to events are generally within reason and acceptable. Understanding your own limitations and personal biases goes a long way toward establishing credibility with your peers.

Here are few tips to improve your reality testing.

Tips & Exercises

Seek other perspectives. When a situation occurs and you are unsure of what meaning to attribute, ask a trusted friend what their take is on it. Brainstorm all of the potential meanings before you come to a conclusion.

Be objective. Try to see a situation from as many angles as possible. When we are quick to make a judgment call on the meaning of a situation we may misread someone's intentions or internalize meaning that is incorrect.

Find or be your own "devil's advocate". By making an argument for something you don't necessarily believe in, you will test the quality of the original argument and identify any weaknesses, and to use such information to either improve or clarify your thought or opposing position.

Ask for feedback from supervisors, coworkers or friends.

Don't think you know what separates reality from illusion. Self-deception is seductive and we all do it to some degree. Try to be objective about yourself, your work situation, and how it fits in the grand scheme of things. Be flexible enough to adjust your thoughts and behaviors accordingly. "When in doubt, check it out". Your final decisions may be more on target if you have collected other points of view.

21

Have an Accountability Partner (AP)

"Accountability" means taking behavioral, intellectual and emotional ownership for the outcomes of what one does. A "partner" is a person who shares or is associated with another in some action or endeavor. An AP then is a person who coaches another person in terms of helping the other person keep a commitment.

One of the best ways to improve your EI is to work with someone outside of your circle who can help you raise your awareness, management and expression of appropriate emotions. An accountability partner is able to perceive what we can't see when blind spots and weaknesses block our vision. Someone whom you trust and is compassionate. We all can benefit from someone who is able to say what we need to hear without making us feel threatened.

If you're married, your spouse should know who your AP is, and your spouse should determine whether he or she wants to be a part of the feedback sessions. It is good to be honest with your wife or husband about your development. However, spouses occasionally can be too close to a sensitive situation to give you constructive feedback. Don't necessarily lean on your spouse for the same kind of support as you do of your AP.

One person might not give you all the support you need, so consider asking more than one person to be your AP.

Here's an example of Sarah and Megan. Sarah wanted to improve her skills in recognizing emotions in others. Megan (AP) and Sarah agreed to meet twice a week - once on Monday and once on Friday by phone. They devoted the Monday meeting to discussing what emotions Sarah would be looking for in others – being careful to only identify 2 or 3. They use the Friday meeting as a time to reflect on the week's observations and discuss Sarah's specific hits and misses.

You and your partner may choose to meet more or less frequently, face to face or e-mail, or set up your meetings differently. Do what works best for you—and do this on a regular basis.

Staying consistent is the key. When you make consistency a priority, meeting with your AP is likely to become a habit -, just like brushing your teeth.

Emotional Intelligence Action Plan (EIAP)

Emotional intelligence is an awareness of your feelings and actions and those of others – and their impact on you and yours on them. This also applies at the individual, group and organizational level. It can include either professional or personal relationships.

Now you can actually develop and enhance the skills that will positively impact your work and personal relationships. Once your current EI been has assessed, the next step is to take action to improve/enhance it. The EIAP will be your "blueprint for enhancing your emotional intelligence. *However, it will only work if you use it.*

Using the EIAP

The EIAP is made up of the following components:

- **Specific Area (s) to Develop** – Clearly state an EI area to enhance, e.g., Empathy, Self-Awareness, Stress Tolerance, Impulse Control.

- **Why? (Objective)** – Identify purpose or reason. By developing/enhancing this area I will… "have a better relationship with my coworker", "be a more effective team player", "reduce my stress level", "have a more optimistic outlook on things".

- **Specific Action to Take** - Specific actions you will take to achieve your goal(s), e.g., take a class in listening; practice counting to 10 before responding when I'm angry, practicing meditation.

- **Resources** – Financial, staff, equipment, etc. needed to accomplish goal. People you will involve in the development process, books, movie clips.

- **Evidence of Change** – Indicators that let you know if the plan was successful in impacting your objective, e.g., feedback from others, able to see both sides of an issue, able to wait longer before responding.

- **Three time periods of 30-day, 60-day and 90-day intervals** - Expected date of completion for each activity/strategy.

During this overall time span, new timeframes and deadlines, new activities, and even new priorities will impact the plan and adjustments might need to be made. Document changes to the plan accordingly, communicate the changes (if working with a coach), and continue to monitor progress toward completion.

<table>
<tr><td colspan="3">Specific Area (s) to Develop:</td></tr>
<tr><td colspan="3">Why? (Objective):</td></tr>
<tr><td colspan="3">30 Day</td></tr>
<tr><td>Specific Actions to Take:

1.

2.

3.</td><td>Resources</td><td>Evidence of Change.</td></tr>
<tr><td colspan="3">60 Day</td></tr>
<tr><td>Specific Actions to Take:

1.

2.

3.</td><td>Resources</td><td>Evidence of Change.</td></tr>
<tr><td colspan="3">90 Day</td></tr>
<tr><td>Specific Actions to Take:

1.</td><td>Resources</td><td>Evidence of Change.</td></tr>
</table>

2. 3.		

About the Author

Hank Clemons, PhD ("Dr. Hank") is founder and President of the Society of Emotional Intelligence, an Emotional Intelligence Coach, Certified Anger Management Specialist-1 and the president of HLC Group, Inc. – a consulting firm located in Tampa, FL. He has over 20 years of experience as a coach and training consultant focusing on Emotional Intelligence and Leadership. He is also a Training Partner with MHS, offering certification in the EQ-i 2.0 & 360.

He has authored several books – Including 7 Steps... Achieving workforce diversity step by step, It Only Takes a Minute, Applying Emotional Intelligence, *From Mail Room to Board Room,* and Could your Emotional Intelligence be Holding you Back?

"Dr. Hank" is the host of a weekly radio show titled "Let's Talk EI". He is a highly sought after speaker often presenting at conferences and special events on emotional intelligence.

Contacting the Author

"Dr. Hank" can be contacted via phone at 813.431.9786 or at hankclemons@gmail.com. He can also be reached via the website of the Society of Emotional Intelligence at: www.societyofei.org

About SoEI
Society of Emotional Intelligence

The Society of Emotional Intelligence was founded in 2009 in response to a growing interest in emotional intelligence. Its vision and mission are as follows.

Vision
Be the premier professional membership driven association for those interested in understanding and applying emotional intelligence in their personal and professional lives as well as the lives of others.

Mission
SoEI is dedicated to increasing the knowledge, ability and application of emotional intelligence of individuals and organizations by providing, conferences, workshops, personal coaching, training and educational programs.

If you are not a member, become a member today!

www.societyofei.org

CPSIA information can be obtained
at www.ICGtesting.com
Printed in the USA
BVHW040819110619
550694BV00011B/101/P

9 781632 635587